It's time to answer your call to be great and do it now.

No regrets.
Take the Leap.
Do what you love.

Have the life you desire.

Table of Contents

Want the audiobook version? As a thank you for getting this book, I'd like to give you the audio version for free. Just go here:

http://bit.ly/freeaudiowhy

Preface

My day started like any other. Laying in bed, I wondered how I would feel when I finally swung my feet over the edge of the bed and they hit the ground. Most days I didn't know what it would feel like being upright. How much pain? What would my head feel like? What hurt? But every day was like this.

I had convinced myself it was ok – that I could muddle through the next 40-some years of the rest of my life like this. I already had plenty of heart-to-heart talks between my heart and my head in the middle of the night. It would be ok. I could keep doing this. Besides, I had a pretty good run the first 40 years of life, right? I'd gotten a good education, had good paying jobs, got married, had kids, owned a home.... This is all we need in life, right? ...... right?

And I asked myself why almost every day. Why did God allow my life to turn out this way? Why had I been destined to be ill? Why was I chosen to endure this kind of life – I couldn't function as a wife, mom, friend (ok, let's be real – the friends really didn't care so they shouldn't even be listed). Supermom has left the building, no longer to show up to every field trip, party, conference …. No more volunteering at church. No more parties either. Everything had consequences – pain and recuperation took five to seven days and the necessities of daily life had to be the priorities.

I had to go get groceries, but when I habitually forgot something in the far corner of the superstore, I wanted to cry. Was it worth it to walk all the way over THERE? Or could we live without? The choice paralyzed me. "I don't think I can make it." So I checked out of the store….. only to find that my mini-van was missing. Almost every time I went to the grocery store just two miles from the house, my anxiety shot up as I went back out to the parking lot. But today, I was really SURE that the mini-van was stolen. It was gone.

I knew for sure I had parked it right there. Or was it over there? Or there? My eyes darted around as I tried to look calm. "Vickie, don't act like a lost 90 year old." (The doctor had actually told me at the last visit to be kind to myself and understand that my body and mind were like a 90 year old's.) I wanted to just REMEMBER where the heck the van was. "Ohmygosh…. I'm going to have to call Mike. The van is really stolen." The tears were about to flow again. "I just can't do this anymore. I'm not going to make it."

And then it finally caught my eye. There. Phew. Thank God I don't need to call anyone.

And this happened about every time I went to the store because the Chronic Lyme Disease bacterial spirochettes had invaded my brain. Seven years of not being diagnosed and ignoring the signs.

Arthritis. Chronic Fatigue. Lupus. Sjogren's. Fibro. And about 20 gazillion other names and labels. But cognitive disorder – COGNITIVE DISORDER - was one of the worst symptoms of the disease. It made me feel dumb. And they only wrote "cognitive disorder" because they didn't want to put "dementia" in a 40-ish's chart, at least that's what the doc told me anyway.

But honestly, the worst part about Lyme Disease is how it rips each part of your life from you, one by one, from activities to depersonalization to brain and heart issues. And little by little you are left with nothing except your own thoughts, just begging God to let you hold out long enough so that your children would be grown up enough to not need you so much.

There comes a day in life, especially if you struggle with something like illness, where you ask yourself if you're willing to go through life like this or if you're going to do something about it. I didn't think I had much control over my destiny and in fact, I was wrong about that. I had much control over how my life was going to pan out.

So I took control. I decided that I was unwilling to live the rest of my life this way, I wasn't going to muddle through and be forgotten when I was gone. I decided that I was put on earth with a meaningful purpose and it was time to figure it out. Never before had I allowed myself to put myself first. This was it! My time was now!

"Now" has turned into an entrepreneurial journey with lessons that I want to share with you here in this book. From my start as a Master Herbalist and wellness coach, changing my focus (what seems like a million times), to becoming a certified business and transformational coach, I've spoken and talked to hundreds of entrepreneurs who desperately want to make an impact and leave the world a better place.

I help my clients to create lives of freedom with businesses that they are excited to get out of bed for. And I include my Law of Attraction practitioner training to increase my client's abilities to manifest what they want in their life and business.

I love to see entrepreneurs get clear on what their true desires are, write a book to help spread the their message and leave a legacy, and in turn get to make their dream life a reality.

Acknowledgement

Thank you to my husband, Mike, who has put up with late nights, listening to my babble, riding the rollercoaster with me, being kicked out of his own space, and letting me fulfill my dreams to be a coach and travel the world while he has to work and takes care of the kids.

This book is dedicated to my children, Stephanie, Nathan and Trenton. I know they have entrepreneurial blood in them and unlimited potential. Don't ever forget you can do and have whatever you desire.

Thank you specifically to my daughter, Stephanie - my sunshine, who has been my biggest fan and cheerleader. I wish I had known what I know now when you were growing up.

Love to my whole family. I love you to pieces!

Introduction

This book is for entrepreneurs: coaches, speakers and authors who want to make an impact, be influential, stand out, be known, create a thriving business, leave a legacy and quit struggling with confusion, lack of direction. This is for those who want to learn how to earn an abundant income while working with ease doing something they're excited and passionate about, with clients they adore.

First, let's talk about that question that never tires in the curiosity of a two year old. It's probably the question we asked the most as a child. "WHY?"

I know it's the one question I remember constantly answering for my children. I was never the mom that minded the questions. I always answered as best I could.

Eventually, we stop asking why though.....

"Because I said so."
"Stop asking that."
"Quit with the why's."
"Curiosity killed the cat."

And we're conditioned to stop wondering and asking, as if it's not good for us or rude.

I've found in my journey of entrepreneurship that this question, "Why?" has been the most important, informative and revealing question I can ask myself. It's the question I ask when I get on discovery calls with my clients. It's what I ask my clients to feel into so they can get grounded.

In fact, I like the question, "Why not?" quite a lot as well.

As you're reading this book, it would be good to have a journal by your side for notes, completing assignments and whatever thoughts come to you. Jot down what hits you. Write out the answers to the questions throughout the chapters. Do the little assignments. Get your mind thinking about all your why's.

The reason I set this book up to be a journaling exercise is because I've found out so many deep things about myself and my entrepreneurial journey, along with the reasons behind my blocks through journaling. Writing things out on paper gets that subconscious conversation going and you can really dive deep into what's holding you back. If you want to get the most out of this book, journal.

As a coach who helps entrepreneurs with manifestation, mindset, marketing, storytelling, law of attraction and writing Best Selling books, I know that writing things out helps you in more ways than you may imagine. You remember things better, even if you never return back to your notes.

I've always been intrigued with what I wrote down last year or even just last month. A little time and growth, then a look back at what you wrote and you'll see how far you've come.

Your why keeps you grounded in your business and your life. If you know your why, you know what you want and when you know what you want, you can then figure out how to get there. Asking, "Why?" is the key to everything. Question always. Answer the why.

Why me?

"Most men lead lives of quiet desperation and go to the
grave with the song still in them."
– Henry David Thoreau

You've been called to be and create a business that reflects what you want in life. I've been called too. We usually ignore it. Or rather, maybe well-meaning adults and friends have shushed us. There's nothing wrong with a three year old wanting to be Superman but there's something wrong with having "unreasonable" dreams about what you want to do when you're grown.

That's not responsible. That's not the way to happiness. That's not the formula. Stick with the formula. Entrepreneurship is too risky. Sound familiar?

I've always wondered where this formula came from and what's odd is that it seems that everyone's heard of the same "Happiness Formula." School + Job + Home + Family = happiness.

I wanted to go to art school but my mother said, "No." Practically speaking, I was going to starve, so I picked something else, Actuarial Mathematics. Yet, when I did that, my mother told me that, "Now everyone is going to hate you for creating high insurance prices." Nothing was ever right. No choice was ever good. There was always a reason it was going to be disaster.

I did it mostly right though – I went to a good school, University of Michigan, got a good corporate job, switched jobs every 2 years to climb that ladder for a nice pay raise, and by the age of 26, I had 6 weeks of vacation, a great benefits package, drove a brand new Infiniti SUV and was Assistant Vice President of the most prestigious department of a large bank.

I made it! I made it! I did it!

The problem was, I wondered almost every night ….. Was this it? That was anti-climactic. THIS is it? Why didn't I feel full and happy?

Something was off. It didn't seem right. My daughter had been just born and she kept getting sick when I put her in daycare. Pneumonia. Bronchitis. Pneumonia. Bronchitis. Back and forth, sleepless nights. Then up for work before the light. Was it worth it? What was I getting? I told my sister, "I can't do this anymore," and a little while later, I quit and then got divorced. I gave up the perfect life. You know, the one in that Happiness Formula that doesn't work.

It seemed I had settled. I had convinced myself that life was meant to pan out this way. I didn't listen to what my heart was saying or how I was feeling. I had gone after it like it was the only way.

What do you feel called to do and be? Do you know that you were meant to leave a mark in this world? Did you know that there are people you are meant to meet and touch? I do. What are you doing about it?

Think of a dam. It blocks water getting from one side to the other. Think of that water as people – those people you're meant to touch. Each day, the water gets blocked up and stopped. It can't go anywhere or do anything. It can't get to the other side because the dam is closed.

Now think of you being on the other side of that dam. While the dam is closed, you're not heeding your call and all those poor people have nowhere to go and don't know what to do. You have a message and a purpose that's meant to be shared with them and you're holding out!

Now think about opening up that dam. THE FLOODGATES! These people are your clients, waiting specifically for you. When you allow the gate to be open, you share your message, you do your special thing, you create that business that you love and you receive those people into your world. You get to help them. They're thankful you finally opened up the gate to let them in and they shower over you. How would that feel?

And then there's the ripple effect. The people you touch will then share and touch the people they know and on and on, over and over ... forever. Whether you touch them with your smile at the grocery store, your Facebook post, your book or their becoming your client, the ripple effect is in place.

I remember when I started to learn more about personal development. I changed. I was less grouchy, moody, on edge. I saw things in a different way. I saw them positively. I was happier and I also complained a lot less.

Now, I come from a long line of complainers. My grandmothers were that way as well. There was always something wrong and I learned even with the good things, there was a bad side. It was always my frame of mind to tear things apart and see where it could be improved before ever thinking anything positively about a task, project or situation. And let me tell you: being grumpy and crabby takes a lot of energy! It's really low vibe.

My daughter had already moved out to college in another state when I was beginning this journey of self-discovery and I was sad that I felt I had lost my chance to influence her or teach her more. But as she saw my posts on Facebook change in tone and she came home to a different mother, with a different outlook, she told me, "I like you better now."
I've affected her and now she calls for chats and advice and she even now calls to tell me what she's shared with her friends. THAT warms my heart. It's the ripple effect.

Do you know the story of Moses? God called him to lead the Egyptians out of Egypt, but Moses made excuses about why he wasn't the right person for the job. Maybe his excuses sound familiar to you.

Moses five excuses:
1. I'm not good enough
2. I don't have all the answers
3. People won't believe me
4. I'm not a good public speaker
5. I'm not qualified

Yeah?

Fear, reluctance, unwillingness…. In the end Moses goes and as he puts one foot in front of the other, he sees his faith grow in what he's been called to do. He also gets help from his bother. And once he gets there, his confidence has grown and he's stepped into the man that God meant for him to be.

What about you? Can you step into being that person you've been called to be?

Listen, you were never meant to be mediocre. You were never meant to live a rinse and repeat life. You were meant for big things. You just have to go for it. Close your eyes. If you censored nothing, what is it that you really want?

What I've found out in my life, and in talking to hundreds of entrepreneurs and coaches, is that until you figure out what lights you up and gets you out of bed each day, you'll feel like something is missing. That's basically because something IS missing in your life.

But only you can answer what it is that's missing. What's that thing that's calling you? Why have you been called to it? Do you have a story to share? Do you have a mission and message that's important to you?

Now, remember that every call involves risk. In order to grow, you have to go where it's an unknown and may seem scary, but remember that if you don't take the risk, you risk living in the torment of "what if".

When you leave your comfort zone to go after and find your calling, it will involve sacrifice as well. You'll leave behind people who don't think like you do. You might not have as much contact with those you love because they don't understand or support where you're going (usually due to their own fears).

With every choice we make, there's a trade off. We will be asked to give up something. You'll be met with resistance and much of it is inside your head.

It could be that we're asked to give up our comfort zone or we could be asked to give up friends, resources or time. But when we choose desire and we choose ourselves, we trade up into a world that we may have never known had we not taken the risk.

The reward for our desires is great. It leads to fulfillment and happiness in a way that we get to define. Wouldn't it be great to wake up excited for your day? Wouldn't it be great to look forward to your work and not feel like it's a chore?

That's where the quote by Marc Anthony, "If you do what you love, you'll never work a day in your life," comes from. I'm sure you've probably heard it. Do you believe it applies to you? Do you think that you're not allowed to do what you love and get well paid for it? Do you think it's wishful thinking and not really possible?

Look around you. There are probably people you know who live that rinse and repeat, mediocre, "drag yourself out of bed" type of life (and think that's all there is). But you know better. You know that there is more out there for you. That's NOT all there is.

Now think about people like Oprah, Louise Hays, Arianna Huffington, or Tony Robbins. Which kind of life would you choose? You want the mediocre? Or do you want the fulfilled life? You've got to answer that call!

If you feel like you're not enough, you're wrong. If you feel like there are too many people in your industry or niche, you're wrong. If you feel like you don't know how to become who you want to be, don't worry.

What do you think is the biggest problem to your being your best, highest self? For most people, it's their mind. Your mind keeps going, telling you all sorts of things like "you're not good enough", "you don't know enough", or "you don't deserve it".

When you step into being your best self, you don't think or feel this way anymore. You feel unlimited potential instead. If you want to feel unlimited potential, then you have to look and take ownership of your own life, becoming aware of what's going on inside and outside of yourself.

Now I invite you to close your eyes, go to a peaceful, safe place and imagine your best self. Feel the experience of being in this place as your best self. What are the qualities of your best self? Confident? Happy? Fulfilled? Free?

Now imagine going through your day as your best self. What are you doing? How are you doing it? How do you solve problems?

Practice communicating with your best self on a conscious level because we subconsciously communicate with it all the time. Ask yourself questions every day and get your answers from your best self. Using these answers will keep you out of conflict with yourself. Then you can show up as your best self, actively participating in your own life.

Any time you come across a problem, ask yourself how your best self would respond. Or if you're not quite sure what you should do next, ask yourself what your best self would do next. And each time you feel that maybe you're not sure you can reach your full potential, ask yourself how you can get there.

You must BE your best self first so that you can DO what your best self would do so that you can HAVE what you want in the end. Most people do this backwards and try to have what they want so that they can do something and then be somebody.

Do you want to be famous? Happy? Successful? Impactful? Influential? Wealthy? Fulfilled? Free? They all have different meanings for different people. But you? You can be whatever you want.

I leave you to answer your why with The Four Fold Franciscan Blessing:

May God bless you with **discomfort**. Discomfort at easy answers, half truths, and superficial relationships, so that you may live deep within your heart. Amen

May God bless you with **anger**. Anger at injustice, oppression and exploitation of people, so that you may work for justice, freedom and peace. Amen

May God bless you with **tears**. Tears to shed for those who suffer from pain, rejection, starvation and war, so that you may reach out your hand to comfort them and turn their pain into joy. Amen

May God bless you with **foolishness**. Enough foolishness to believe that you can make a difference in this world, so that you can do what others claim cannot be done. Amen

Author's Note:

In case you are one of those people who skip introductions to books, I want to explain briefly again why journaling is so important. I used to not enjoy journaling because I didn't want to come face to face with my true feelings and thoughts. Going there wasn't safe in my world. I couldn't be strong if I allowed feelings. And even though I'm quite intuitive and feel a lot with my heart and gut, I didn't want to do this.

Instead, I envied those who could and did. I wanted to be like them and yet I couldn't.

It was only when I forced myself to start doing it that I realized how much of I opened up by putting pen to paper. It became so revealing and enjoyable. It was like a conversation with God and the Universe that was true, raw, safe and all me.

It's not just about writing though – you don't have to be a good or even a decent writer to journal. You just have to be open to wanting the transformation that happens when you do it.

When you journal, it forces you to think clearly. There's something about translating your feelings and thoughts into words that's magical. When you translate that energy into words, it allows your mind to really wrap around things that you may not have been able to really express or even knew was in there. The free-flow of journaling really allows you to get it all out.

Things becomes clear. It's you, your imagination, your best self ... everything about your thoughts are brought to life. It identifies things that you may not have allowed to be in your conscious awareness. Expressing your emotions into a journal helps you to "get things out" in a safe space and in the end, I promise, it will change your life.

Journal Assignment:

What do you feel called to?

What kind of business would you love to have?

Did you have something you wanted to be or do when you were young but you were told it was wrong? What was it? Do you still want to do it?

Who is the person you've been called to be? Can you describe him or her?

Draw yourself as your biggest, best self.

Why You Push Success Away

"In my life I've discovered that if I cling to the notion that something's not possible, I'm arguing in favor of limitation.
And if I argue for my limitations, I get to keep them."
- Gay Hendricks, The Big Leap

It may seem inconceivable to you that you'd push any type of success away, but it's actually pretty common.

When you get to a certain point in your life, whether it's in a relationship or business, there comes a time where you may consciously or subconsciously ask, "Am I allowed to be this successful, happy or wealthy?" and "Can I have this amount of abundance in my life?"

The next thing that happens is a bit of self-sabotage. Have you noticed that when your business is going super well, you get into a fight with your partner or kids? Or if you're really happy with your love life, your business seems to have issues?

Maybe it's just a general thing where when things seem to be going really well, you all of the sudden start to get crabby and annoyed with silly things?

According to Gay Hendricks in <u>The Big Leap</u>, this is an "upper limit" problem. The upper limit problem is like that glass ceiling that you aren't allowed to go past. This mostly has to do with our beliefs about what we are allowed to have. Whatever it is, we can't have THAT much of it: happiness, success, wealth, fun, ease, love, etc.

When we start getting close to "it", we self-saboage in order to back off and stay in our comfort zone. This is part of having a fear of success (and it can be a part of fear of failure as well). You have an internal thermometer and it tells you, "WHOA!" you've never been this close before. Back off. You're not allowed here.

Before I learned about this, I had no idea that it was even possible to sabotage myself in this way.

When I was studying to become a Divine Living Certified Business and Transformational Coach, we were required to record 100 hours of coaching, 70 of which had to be paid coaching hours. Time was getting short and I was losing confidence each day that I would get my hours in in time. I just didn't see how it was possible or even probable when the hours for each day didn't add up well in my head.

I started to convince myself that I didn't need to be certified, that it was ok if I didn't get the certification, and that I didn't need to prove anything to anyone. Defiance.

What I was really doing was letting myself down easy.

The conversation in my head was that it was easier for me to decide I didn't have the desire to graduate rather than go through all the stress, try and fail. If I made this conscious decision to stop trying, then I was in control.

Was it really true for me? Was I really in control? Or was I letting fear get to me? Did it really not matter to me?

Once I realized that my truth was that I wanted to graduate, and that I wanted the hours, but that I was scared, I was able sell and finish the hours required. It wasn't nearly as hard as I had imagined in my head. Sure there were weeks that I coached for 18 hours, but it was worth it. I did it and I conquered it and I know I could do it again if I had to. Now that upper limit has moved on up higher because I passed the ceiling.

I know now I'm allowed to have that level of success, achievement and happiness. I also know what it feels like to have that level of success as well. Feeling that success is the key to getting more successes like it.

When you feel success, you have to anchor it in. The reason is that the more you focus on success in any form, the more you're working with the Law of Attraction.

The Law of Attraction states that like attracts like and uses the magnetic power of The Universe to help you to create and manifest what happens in your life. You can manifest positive things or you can manifest negative things and the great thing is, it's your choice.

When you feel success and anchor it in, you are able to create that feeling again. That feeling place helps you attract it. The more you can feel something, the more you can attract it. And once you know how to do this, you become a deliberate creator. You co-create with the Universe and God. It's pretty amazing. You can create whatever you want. What is your heart's desire?

Five Steps to Anchoring in Your Success

1. Allow yourself to see your success as success – many times we don't allow ourselves to consider something that we've done worthy of celebration. Success comes in sizes from tiny to extra large. Allow all of them to be a celebratory occasion.
2. Give yourself credit – give yourself the gift of seeing yourself as the creator of your success. You did it and no one can take it away from you.
3. Attach a muscle memory to your success – give yourself a fist pump, cheer, happy dance, or whatever comes natural to you when you're excited about a win. This gets the feeling into your body and the muscle memory will come again with the next success.

4. Connect your success to your heart – feel your success deeply in your heart. Remember how it feels. Close your eyes and feel into it. How you connect with your success will help you connect with more success.
5. Expand your success – imagine your success even bigger. What if you had even more success that you have right now? How would that feel? How would this success be even better? How much more will you allow into your life. Think of an expanding circle. Grow the circle and grow your feeling of being successful.

The great thing about your successes is that if you can create it once, you can create it again, plus more. Start with the small things. Celebrate them. The feeling place will help you attract even more. The more you can feel it, the more you will attract it.

When people ask me how I get my clients, I answer that I simply call them in. At first when I started to do this, my belief was small. I believed the Law of Attraction, but I also didn't think that I could have it all. I had a problem receiving what was being sent to me. I didn't think I deserved it.

There was a bit of lip service quite honestly, but as I saw small successes, I realized how much truth there was and my belief grew into pure trust. I wanted to work WITH the Law of attraction so that I could have more ease in my life and business.

I remember my first group launch for my Easy Writer: Guaranteed Amazon Group Program. I didn't really know the proper way to launch a group program. I had just thrown some offers out there, did a webinar two months too early, and thought I could get 25 people into my group. I had a plan, but I constantly second guessed it because I didn't have any guidance.

About 12 days prior to the program start, I asked the Universe for two more people to join the group in the next three days because the prep module was starting then. Before falling asleep, I visualized these two people. I thanked God for already sending them to me. I imagined messages in Facebook. Opened my arms up to receiving them and fell asleep.

Note: I do this before bed because your subconscious mind works while you're asleep. It doesn't now truth from fiction, so planting this seed helps the Universe to make it happen.

When you're focused on abundance, nothing is impossible. You get to decide how much abundance comes in and when.

When you focus on lack such as looking at what's wrong, feeling like you're not worthy, competing and comparing with others, thinking that you have to work hard, push and struggle for everything, feeling that you have to fight for your share, thinking your success is limited, blaming, procrastinating, thinking that The Universe and God is only supporting you some of the time, and thinking only of the problems, then lack is what you'll get more of.

Remember that every successful person didn't start out that way. There was very likely a breakdown (multiple breakdowns) before any turning point that released to them the knowing more of their higher, better, true self, along with honing in on their calling and desires.

Journal Assignment:

How can you be more grateful throughout your day?

In what ways can you turn your non-productive thoughts around?

How have you been using the Law of Attraction without knowing it? What things in the past have you manifested?

In what ways can you become more of a deliberate creator?

What action are you going to begin to attach to your successes, no matter how small?

Write your abundance declaration and include what you desire more abundance in, how you'll create more abundance in that area, how you'll celebrate, and how it feels to receive it.

Want more on attracting abundance in your life? Get my Best Selling book, "Standing in the Gap: 40 days to becoming a deliberate creator of abundance in your life" on Amazon at https://www.amazon.com/dp/B06W9L9 8GW

Why desire?

"To burn with desire and keep quiet about it is
the greatest
punishment we can bring on ourselves."
— Federico García Lorca

Most of us have been told since we were
young to put others first. That equates to
rarely saying "yes" to ourselves. Being
sacrificial became a highly respected quality,
so to feel good, we went after it.

It's also a respected quality to deny yourself.
You can be super proud of yourself to have the
self discipline to keep away from those
cookies! Denying ourselves has become
normal, commonplace and expected.

You hear it all the time. Wait until later. Not
now. You can do without. Make do with what
you have. Did you know that these
statements are made from a place of lack?
You feel like you won't have more later, so
you'll settle for what you have now. Not
wanting more is unnatural. We were created
with desires so don't make yours wrong.

Becoming a parent became the ultimate sacrificial example for me. I showed up at every field trip, every party, every practice and every game. It became my identity to be called "superwoman" because I was always there for everyone …. except me.

I worked over 40 hours per week, took the kids to their activities, volunteered at church, even set aside time to paint there, cooked a meal from scratch and proudly worked some more in the evenings after the kids went to bed.

"Overachiever" and "Type-A" were labels I loved. I wore the badge proudly. Every time someone said it, I felt good about myself and what I'd achieved.

What I had I really achieved though? Where was I in this life? Where did I fit in? And what was the purpose of all this? I didn't know.

Once I became an entrepreneur, I did what I thought I was supposed to do. Even my vision board was filled with things I thought were supposed to be there. I denied myself even when I thought I wasn't denying myself anymore because I made what I wanted wrong.

What did I want?

I've always wanted to be famous. There I said it. Am I going to be judged for it? Of course I am! But guess what? We are all being judged one way or another, so why not be judged for your true heart's desire?

Now, wishing is different than desires. When you wish, you're fantasizing and when you fantasize, you don't really believe it's going to come true. It becomes a it-would-be-nice-if kind of thing. This holds true not just for wishing, but hoping. Those have a safety net under them because there's no expectation of them coming true.

Now, desires, those are different. You have the power to make your desires come true. Don't worry though, your desires don't have to make sense right now. You don't need to see how to get to the end, but we tend to block those things because we want to know how it's going to happen. Do you need a plan all laid out in front of you? The Universe doesn't work that way. While God has a bird's eye view on your exact trek through the maze, you're down in the trenches unable to see over the walls and bushes.

Trust. That's it. You've got to trust you can have it and that you'll get there. Faith. It's what will keep you going.

You belief system may challenge your desires and holds you back from going after it. Can you really have that? Is it allowed? Is it possible?

Sometimes you don't get to live your desires because you don't ask for enough (it's that safety thing). Don't you want to be that success story? I know I do. Remember your own power. Your thoughts mold your life and what can and will happen for you. If you open yourself up to the possibilities, rather than the probabilities, then you'll see what can be yours. Why not make defying the odds normal for you?

And the thing is, what you desire is already yours. It's waiting for you to claim it. You just have to believe and go get it.

Here's the big thing though: don't think that your desires are based on what you can do right now. Just because you have the skills for something doesn't mean you're meant to do it or that it's your calling. You just have skills.

In fact, you can have mad skills at something and it's still not your calling, you've just practiced really hard and have gotten super good at something. Great! But don't mistake that for your calling. And don't feel stuck in it because you've invested a lot of time in getting really good at it. Is it worth doing if it's not what makes you happy?

You get to decide what you spend your time and brain power on. What is THAT thing that you'd do regardless if you had to or not? What would you do with your free time if you could fill it with what you loved?

I've been one of those "lucky" entrepreneurs who didn't have to make money. I have a roof over my head, my children are clothed and fed. My husband has a good job. I didn't come from the same place as others who had lost their jobs or were single moms who felt like they had to make it work so they could survive. If you think it's an easier place to come from, it's not necessarily what you think. I wrote about it in Huffington Post in 2016 here:
http://www.huffingtonpost.com/vickie-gould/the-biggest-obstacle-to-y_b_9684892.html

According to Tony Robbins, we operate on 6 human needs. These are the driving force behind what we do and how we act. Knowing that fame is important to me, it's probably not too surprising that my top human need is significance. What's yours?

The six human needs are:

Love and Connection
Certainty
Uncertainty or Variety
Significance
Contribution
Growth

The first four are important drivers in your life. Everyone has all these needs, but in different orders of importance. What we do feeds our need for these six human needs and determines what we strive for.

Knowing the order of your six human needs helps you understand your why. It also helps you to see the flip side to some of those needs that can sabotage your success. For example, if you really strive for certainty, like my husband who will buy the same pair of shoes over and over after the first pair has worn out because he knows exactly what he's getting, then anything that throws you out of that comfort zone can cause havoc in your life. If you're like me and enjoy significance, Tony says you may end up surrounding yourself with people under your level so that you can feel better about yourself.

Back to that vision board: I put all the things that every other coach was talking about like bigger homes, nicer cars, fancy clothes, vacations. I made it into something like a graded school project and didn't even realize it until almost a year later. I hung it on my wall, looked at it every day and felt nothing.

Because it wasn't a reflection of my true desires.

It wasn't that all the things on my vision board were not my desires. It was more like my true top desires weren't even on it at all. I remember coming back from a live event and realizing how un-representative my vision board was so I took it down and started over. I allowed myself to put things on it like being on Oprah, walking down the red carpet, being on a magazine and WOW, what a difference alignment makes!

A while later, I learned about goal mapping from a friend and that stepped it up a notch more. Goal mapping requires you to draw out your desires, instead of cutting out photos of things. When they're coming straight from your imagination onto paper, it's even more powerful because you have to actually see you as "it" or "there" in your mind's eye before you can draw it.

On that goal map, I put "World Class Speaker" and "Impacting the World" and drew out exactly what that looked like. It really helped me to feel into what I truly desired and it felt good to finally tell myself that it was ok to want what I wanted.

No matter what drives you and what your desires are, knowing your desires is what's going to keep you going when things get tough. Your desires give you the reason and the motivation, so make sure you're asking yourself the deep questions. And keep asking until you uncover the truth of your real, true desires.

"I don't want realism. I want magic!" - Tennessee Williams, A Streetcar Named Desire

When you do the journal assignment below, make sure you ask yourself, "Why?" enough times. Not continuing until the last answer is going to leave you hanging.

When I used to be a wellness coach, I would ask people why they wanted to lose weight. The answer generally was because they wanted to be healthier. Valid answer, but there's more. Ask, "Why?" again and the answer was so they could feel better. Ask, "Why?" again and the answer might be so they could be a better mom. Keep asking and you'll get even more.

If you're a coach, when your client starts to give up or flounder, bringing them back to their desires and their why will get them back on track with their vision. Once they're back "on" with their vision, they can get the motivation they need to continue on past the tough times.

This holds true for you too. Knowing your deep desire and why will help keep you grounded when you run over rough patches or feel like spending a day watching Netflix, drowning your sorrows in mint chocolate chip ice cream.

Author's Note:

Are you proud to say you have no desires, that you have everything you could ever want in life? There's a difference between being thankful for what you have and not having desires.

Sometimes saying you don't have desires comes from a place of lack. Perhaps you think that you don't deserve it. Perhaps you think it's not possible. Or maybe you think you can't create what you desire.

There's no getting around the fact that we all have desires. Many of us have been conditioned to believe they're wrong; however, we naturally want to grow and manifest more in our lives.

Remember that whatever you ask for is already on its way. Your jobs is to have the faith of a mustard seed because your desires are there waiting for you. It's available. It's already been created and you have to just allow yourself to get in alignment with it. When you're on that same level and it's the right time, then it'll be yours to claim.

Journal Assignment:

What are the order of your six human needs?

Without squashing it down or making it wrong, what do you truly desire from your life?

Draw it out.

Why do you choose this? What would it do for you and your loved ones? Now ask yourself why you want that and why you want the next answer and why you want the next answer even (at least 3 times) until you get to the real truth of what you desire.

I'd love to hear what you've gotten so far out of your journaling. Share what you've uncovered so far in my

http://www.facebook.com/groups/bethe realdeal

Why now?

"You don't have to be great to start, but you have to start to be great." - Zig Ziglar

Do you think that now isn't the right time? Think you have to do a few other things or get something "out of the way" before you can create a business that you love? Or maybe you've started your business and there's something you'd like to do with it that you're waiting on the right moment. Got an idea that you think you'll do "later?"

Well, there will always be a reason you can find for why now isn't the "best time." Whether it's an imperfect website, waiting for the kids to get older, losing a little weight or wanting to get more education, it's time to get comfy with the idea that there's never going to be the perfect time, but there WILL be a time that you'll have regrets if you don't do this now.

When I was sick, I spent about four years wondering if I'd ever get better. Early on, I had a lot of determination. I still tried to be superwoman. But as the years went on, and it seemed like I was getting worse instead of better, the hope started to flicker. I'd lie awake at night, staring at the ceiling in the dark and I wasn't sure that I'd ever feel well enough to travel, play with my future grandchildren or even survive a trip to the mall.

It was on those nights that I would lay in bed or cry on the cold bathroom floor that the regrets would flood over me. All the things I wished I had done, all the people I'd let treat me poorly, all the times I'd pushed my wants aside, thinking the sacrificial thing made me a better person.

None of that mattered anymore. All I could think about was the fact that I never did what I wanted. I never stood up for what my heart told me. I squelched myself. I let my head convince me out of having anything for myself. I made what I wanted wrong. And that in itself was wrong.

You matter and that means that what you want matters.

Don't keep waiting and putting off what you know you'd love to be doing with your life and business. Waiting longer not only impacts you, but also the world – the people you're supposed to help.

Do you think it doesn't matter or that someone else will step in to make up for the void that's your place? Think again. Remember that dam? Those people are waiting for you and only you can fill that place of what they need.

It's also urgent. Procrastination is the killer of dreams. It comes from a place of lack. Putting things off can be from feelings of lack of confidence, lack of ability, lack of time, lack of deservability, lack of belief, lack of perfection, and lack of desire. It's a form of self-punishment and an addiction to self-pity. It keeps you in the low vibration of struggle.

If you want to be a deliberate creator of your life, you have to take control of it and not let your life just happen to you. Let it happen for you and with you.

You weren't put on this earth to live a mundane, mediocre, rinse and repeat life, were you? I don't think so. We all have a divine purpose. There is a reason for our existence. We are meant to touch certain people in the world and when we don't step into who we are truly supposed to be, those people miss out … immensely. And so do we.

It's your time, so take your turn in life and do what you want. Block out the nay-sayers, the pessimists, the people who think they're saving you from yourself (really, it's a reflection of them, not you). It's time to go for it! No regrets.

Journal Assignment:

What would you regret if you didn't do?

Why is now the best time for you?

What would you allow to stand in your way? Why?

Why Your Wealth Consciousness Makes or Breaks Your Business

"Abundance is not something we acquire. It's something we tune into." – Wayne Dyer

What you think about money in your personal life and your business will determine how much of it you make AND how easily it comes to you. It's not about being rich. It's about being abundant in a way that allows you to be your best self and live the life you were meant to live. You will need funds to achieve your dreams and touch those lives you were meant to touch.

This is why your money story is one of the most important things to explore if you want to create and achieve the level of abundance you're looking for in your business and life.

What have you learned about money from your mother? Your father?

My mother grew up poor, in Taiwan. There were five children in her family, they lived in a small home, and they sucked the marrow out of chicken bones because there wasn't enough food.

She was a very hard worker, such a hard worker that her mother said if she had been born a boy, she would've been all set (the boys take care of the parents as they age in the Asian culture). All her life, they never had money and she had to work for everything she wanted.

After she married my father, they moved from Taiwan to Canada, where my dad got his Ph.D., they came with barely any money between them. My mom had big dreams that they would be wealthy, but soon, they didn't have anything left between them and my father's small stipend for his Ph.D. program wasn't enough for the two of them and their new baby (my sister).

My mother ended up becoming a seamstress to help out. As the story goes, she had to finish up a dress for a customer as I was being born and because of it, they almost didn't make it to the hospital in time before I came.

She was always worried there wouldn't be enough. She gave up eating so that my sister and I would have food. She sacrificed everything she wanted in order to give us a life she didn't have. All the money "stuff" put a big stress on her body and mind and she was constantly on edge.

And there was always tension in the home because my Dad didn't stress about money. He had the philosophy that if there wasn't money, "You just make more," and this really upset my mother. She wanted enough, plus extra to feel safe. She shopped the clearance racks, taught me to be frugal and showed me how to save money at every turn by doing things for yourself. When you couldn't do it all, she taught me how to haggle, search for deals and coupons and get things for the best price possible so that there would be enough for something else that might come up later, just in case.

So what I learned was that money requires hard work. Remember how "money doesn't grow on trees?" I learned that too. I also learned that saving money and having a nest egg meant safety and security. Not having it meant worry, stress and feeling anxious about ... well, everything.

What about having too much? Being wealthy?
That meant that people would look at me like I
was a snob and think I wasn't humble. It also
meant that I would be asked to give money
away to people just because I had it, not
because I wanted to.

How about you? Any of these things sound
familiar? Strike a chord? Are they the same
things that are in the way of you being truly
abundant in your business and life?

Well, none of it is true. For the most part,
what we've been taught about money isn't
true. It doesn't have to be hard and elusive.
We don't turn into evil snots if we have it and
we get to choose what we do with it and who
we give it to when we have it.

You have a choice now. You can continue to
think things like the above or you can replace
these false ideas with new ones and play big.
And if you had more wealth, who better in the
world to use that money responsibly than you?

Knowing that your wealth consciousness also
dictates how well you sell your products and
packages is crucial to getting new clients.

I had a client who, prior to our working together, couldn't sell her coaching package at $100/hour. She thought it was reasonable and having come from a teaching background, she felt it was a step up from her previous position. Her past programming told her that she wasn't worth more.

However, month after month, she'd speak to people and never had anyone sign up. She couldn't understand why. She thought is was such a great deal that everyone would be happy to sign up. She was starting to get frustrated when she decided to talk to me.

The first thing I asked her was why she priced her package at the $1200 price for 12 sessions. Her answer was that it seemed like what everyone else was doing and that someone else had told her to set her price there.

Now see, she'd done plenty of hours upon hours of free coaching which she got rave reviews for, but never got paid for it. She couldn't understand where all the clients were because she knew she had something special to give at a steal.

The problem wasn't in the logic surrounding her package pricing. The problem was that it wasn't enough. She was worth more than $100/hr and deep inside she knew it. When I asked her if she wanted to sell a package at $1200 for 90 days, her answer was, "no." It didn't feel good and she felt like she would resent coaching someone at that price. BINGO!

As soon as she raised her price to $2000, she felt so great, was so relieved, and felt aligned with her price. The dread lifted, her voice was excited when she talked about her packages and she was way more confident sharing what she did.

Do you tell yourself you're not worth what you know deep down you want to charge? Do you squeak out your package price because you're not confident about it for whatever reason? Do you ever tell yourself that money is for other people and not for you?

Here are 7 universal truths about money that I learned from Joe Vitale.

1. Money likes freedom - Money has no beliefs about you like you have about it.

2. Money likes speed. (Speedy action) This means when you get an idea, it's a gift from The Universe to act on.
3. Money likes appreciation – It likes you to be thankful for it. Gratitude creates a high vibration and is an attraction factor.
4. Money likes attention – It likes you to think about it, positively.
5. Money likes energy - Your energy. Your health. Your happiness. Money is attracted to all of that.
6. Money likes to circulate. This is called "prosperous spending". There is also "prosperous purchasing". Money likes to come back to you. When you purchase something you bless someone with money and it will come back to you.
7. Money likes respect - Money is not evil. Money doesn't want to be thought of poorly.
8. Money likes a mission – Money likes to know its purpose, so you should name where your money is going so that it knows the reason you need it.

When you start to think about money differently, can you feel you energy shift? Is it more open and relaxed?

Journal Assignment:

Write out your money story from your mom.

Write out your money story from your dad.

If it would feel good to you, release those stories by burning them in a safe place, cutting them up, or throwing them away.

Rewrite your truths about money.

Listen to free audio training on wealth consciousness:
https://s3-us-west 2.amazonaws.com/easywritergroupprogr am/wealth+consciousness+training+Eas y+Writer+Bonus.mp3

Want to work more on your money story? Get this free workbook and print out your free pocket cards:
https://s3.amazonaws.com/freebiesfrom vickie/Transform+Your+Money+Story.pd f

Why You Must Share Your Story

"The best teachers are the best storytellers.
We learn in the form of stories."
- Frank Smith

We all have lives. We all have stories.
They're meant to be shared. We live. We
learn. We share. We teach. We help.

Our lives are meant for something. What we
go through is meant for something too.
Whether good or bad, the journey of our lives
helps the next person we talk to about it.
What we go through is what we coach on. It's
ok to share whatever it is because it's your
story and it belongs to you.

Your clients buy identities. When you tell your
story, they relate to you. When you share
that you've been where they are and have
come out on the other side, they want your
solution too. The outcome is exactly what
they've been searching for.

What are the lessons you can teach people
from your stories? This is the key to how you
get paid. Your stories touch on their secret
desires.

People also love to feel included or be part of a group or a mission. When you share your story, they get to see a part of themselves in you. They also want to be a part of your mission. They BUY IN.

If you want to engage someone, tell a story – they're fascinating. And they create a fascination factor for you.

I left my home when I was 17, after having an all-out brawl on the kitchen floor with my mother. As usual, when we had our biggest fights, my father wasn't home. She pulled my hair by the fistful. I pulled hers back. She grabbed my arm and left a hand print bruise on my arm. My head was throbbing, and I ran to my room.

Slammed the door.

Packed my things in my school backpack.

I used bungee cords to slide down the wall of my second story window and left my home. It was scary because they stretched with my weight and I was afraid to fall to the ground but I made it safely. It was pitch black dark and I could barely see as I crossed the neighbor's back lawn. It was a little chilly, but not too cold and it was about to storm. I barely remember how I got to the overly bright gas station across from our subdivision to call my friend to pick me up.

I realized later that I had brought my schoolbooks and my contact lens solution but I didn't bring any underwear. Well, at least I had everything I needed to show up to school the next day.

The following weeks were a blur as I jumped around to friends' homes and went to school. It was my senior year and it was supposed to be fun.

I had no idea what I was doing and was thankful to be fed each day by someone's parents who cared enough to take me in. I didn't have a permanent place to stay. It was a little bit of an adventure and funny thing was, I really didn't worry about it. The other funny thing was that my grades were better, not that they were bad, but you know ….

There was less than a half a year of school left and then I'd be going to college after the summer, so I continued to go to my after school job and bought a blue 5 speed stick shift Toyota Celica. Then in the summer, I got my first apartment. It had a mattress in the bedroom, my best friend bought me some kitchen towels and I ate dinner like a picnic on the carpeted floor.

I knew I could get through and though it was hard to be on my own, it was also the best time in my life. I was free, I could make my own choices and I felt like I was finally able to stop being on edge.

So see? There are a lot of stories that you can share:

Your core story: Sharing your why. What's the lesson you learned that you want to teach people? What problem can you help fix in the world?

Human story: sharing when you messed up and failed. BE YOURSELF. SHOW your human side. BE REAL.

Case studies: success stories of yours, your clients or famous people.

Your story becomes your secret sauce. It shows people that you know what you're talking about and when you share your story properly, your prospect will never ask you about your credentials, schooling or require proof that you can help them. They know already that you can purely through the life you've lived. And now they know you and like you.

The key to making your story engaging is to make it vulnerable. This is the human factor that many want to gloss over. Almost all my clients think this this part "isn't interesting" and people won't want to hear it, but it's the most important part. Funny thing is that it's also the most interesting part as well.

Vulnerability sells. It's a deep connection. It's showing you trust the person you're telling the story to. In return, they trust you too.

Did you see what just happened? The know, like and trust factor that we have grown to understand creates life-long clients just happened through story.

<u>Journal Assignment</u>:

When you introduce yourself and someone asks you what you do, which story would you share about why?

How can you find vulnerability comfortable?

Where are all the places that you can share your story?

Want to find out how to create a magnetic story that you can leverage for bigger exposure and visibility for your business? Learn to use the 4 must-have components in your stories.

Especially for you only, use the code: **WHY** to get over 50% off of my $49 Story course valued at $600 for just $24 here: http://member.vickiegould.com/story-course-home/

Why Writing a Book is the Right Next Step for Your Business

"What really knocks me out is a book that, when you're all done reading it, you wish the author that wrote it was a terrific friend of yours and you could call him up on the phone whenever you felt like it.
That doesn't happen much, though."
- J.D. Salinger

When you've gotten to a point in your business where you want more credibility, expert status, influence, impact and the ability to raise your prices, write a book. Really, when is it not a good time for these things? You always need to keep upping the ante. A book is the ultimate in marketing connection and growing your reach.

You've got to have the right kind of book though. It needs to be easily consumed (short read), it has to be able to lead the reader back to you to become your client (lead magnet), and it has to be a best seller. When you have the right kind of book, it becomes the right next step.

If you're writing a book because you just want a place to put your thoughts down forever, that's ok if you don't want clients from it.

If you're writing a book purely because you want to say you wrote one, that's ok too if you don't want clients from it.

If you're writing a book and want to turn those readers into clients, it's got to be structured correctly for its purpose as well: the dual purpose of giving the reader lots of value and creating clients for your coaching business.

Here's what a book can give you:

1. A LEAD MAGNET – it has to have things in it that allows the reader to understand that you're in business and can be their personal coach. This is how you get people interested in you and your business and it builds your list.

2. LEVERAGE - the added clout and credibility, social proof will make you not only stand out but crush the competition. Just think about it - if you were choosing 2 completely equal services or coaches, wouldn't you choose the one that's got a best selling book?

3. EXPERT STATUS - if people don't see you as an expert, you'll always be commanding newbie coach prices. You don't want that do you? "A best-selling book just makes people look at you differently. People see me as someone who knows more than my competition." (quote from a past client)

In addition, if you're looking to be a speaker, a book is a must. Conference coordinators basically expect it these days with as simple as it is to self-publish. A book commands respect and a higher price.
I've even heard from a client before that one of the reasons they wanted to write their book because the last speaking event coordinator was willing to pay double the speaking fee to those with a book. DOUBLE. The price was $5000 versus $10,000. That's big, just for having a book, isn't it?

When I was in elementary school, I read the whole children's public library, literally. Every week I would borrow the maximum 10 books and read most of the day after school. My mother liked to see me reading, though she called them "junk" books because they weren't textbooks and it kept me out of trouble with her.

Reading was my way of escaping my life. I remember the soft, tan curved and tufted chair I would sit sideways in while I read. It was right by the living room window where I could look outside and see our cherry blossom tree.

While I read, I lived other people's lives and lived their adventures. I learned from the things they went through and I solved mysteries in their lives. I became the characters in those books. It helped me to grow up and be able to see so many things from other perspectives.

Sometimes I learned about history, like in Little House on the Prairie and sometimes I lived out childhood adventures like in Ramona the Great. Every story I read gave me insights and new knowledge about something. Every new book was a new experience that I welcomed into my life.

The book that you write, just like this one you're reading now will be a way to share your life and adventures, your learnings and perspectives, to people who need your help. You will share your message, further your impact and influence, and be able to live forever in your book. You will have an ongoing way to communicate with people that you may never had been able to reach and this is the one of the best reasons to write your book.

Back in High School, I was editor of everything in school: the yearbook, the literary magazine, the newspaper. I was editor of everything that had to do with publishing something with words. Looking back, it makes total sense now what I do helping people write and monetize their books, along with publishing my own online magazine called Real Deal™ Magazine.

Remember that ripple effect? A book is a prime example of how you help create it. When you step up and do what you're called to do, create that message you want to share, and have a mission to take it to the people you're meant to touch in a book, guess what happens? Your book will get passed around. Your words will get shared.

People will talk about how your book has impacted their life. What they learn from your book will help them to help others. They pass on the knowledge. And those people pass that on. You may never know those people four levels or even 100 levels from you, but know that they'll be there.

Oh, and if you think you have to be a master of English, it's absolutely not true. It's not English class; it's not graded. There are sentences in this book that aren't sentences. Have you noticed? People want to hear YOU in your book. They want to read as if they're listening to you talk to them. Don't treat it like an assignment. Treat it like two friends over coffee talking.

I know how much words influence. I know how much connection matters and I know that books are the ultimate way to get your message out. You get to live forever in books. Now it's your turn.

Journal Assignment:

What would you want to write about in your book?

Do you have a secret sauce that you need to share?

What's the message you'd like to send to the world?

Who would you want to read your book? Does it match up to your ideal client?

What was the last book you recommended to someone? Why? Why would someone recommend your book?

What's the deadline date for your book?

Now look at your deadline date again. Is it far off? If so, what are you avoiding?

Want to find out the shortcuts on how to write your book quickly and easily? First, take a fun quiz about if you're a right or left brained writer and then get the FREE Guide afterwards (plus a lot of other bonuses) right here: http://vickiegould.com/left-right-brained-writer/

Why the Level of Your Connection = the Level of Your Success

"We cannot live only for ourselves. A thousand fibers connect us with our fellow men; and among those fibers, as sympathetic threads, our actions run as causes, and they come back to us as effects."
- Herman Melville

Being connected is something that we all want. We need relationships. We need other people, just like after God made Adam and then said in Genesis 2:18, "It is not good that the man should be alone; I will make him an help meet for him." And there came Eve so that Adam would not walk the earth by himself.

Most entrepreneurs and coaches have a desire to help the world in some way. We want to make an impact on mankind, big or small. We want to leave our mark. We have a heart for people.

The better we are at connecting, the more we can influence and the more we can make an impact. And if you want impact, that equals your success.

Connection is risky though. It opens you up to feel and be hurt, but it is only in connections that we can truly relate.

As Jay Conrad says in Guerilla Marketing, "If you can talk to them about themselves, you'll have their full attention." We all love being the center of attention any time we can.

These days we know that marketing is about relationships. Create a good bond and a common ground and you have the formula for success.

Get to that place of connection and you can sell anything. Now, I'm not encouraging you to be fake. Of all things, please don't be a fake because people can smell that a mile away. Don't even be tempted to try it. It just doesn't work.

True connection comes from within and it's that heart-tie that you can feel when you meet someone and the conversation goes so well you feel like you've known them forever.

I met my husband on a jet plane (sounds better than commercial airline, doesn't it?). Every time I tell this story, he rolls his eyes as if I exaggerate and I absolutely don't. Not. One. Bit.

I spied him across the aisle from my seat. I noticed he had advertisements from the newspaper strewn across his flip-down tray and somehow I found that endearing. It was nearing Christmas and to have a guy looking through ads for presents seemed so sweet. Then I saw that he had the same notebook I had. I was on a business trip to St. Louis for training on being a stock broker and he had the same notebook for homework that I had under those ads. But the other thing I noticed was that his notebook was blank. He hadn't done his assignment.

I figured I should leave him alone so he could finish his assignment, so I didn't talk to him until we landed.

I stood up and said, "Looks like we're going to the same place." I don't recall what he said, but we continued to chat and walked through the terminal together.

I happen to hate going to baggage claim, so I had packed everything in my carry-on; however, he had not, so to be polite, I followed him to baggage claim before we caught the shuttle to our hotel.

"Great. I shouldn't have talked to him. I don't want to go to baggage claim," I thought to myself. But I smiled and walked.

As we road the moving sidewalk past a glass smoking room (I don't even think that's legal now anymore), we talked about how much we disliked smoking when, BAM!, the end of the sidewalk. And he almost fell on his face. I tried to hold in my laughter since we had just met, but it was really hard.

Once we arrived at baggage claim, we continued to talk while he kept an eye out for his bag. Then the conveyor belt stopped. His bag wasn't there. "Oh, just fantastic," I thought. "I didn't even want to be here and now I'm going to be here longer. I just want to go to the hotel and chill."

Again, to be polite, I went with him to the airline desk to report the luggage lost, only to find out we had been standing at the wrong conveyor belt! Finally to the shuttle and the hotel.

He talked the whole time there, even though he said he wasn't much of a talker. He had something about him that made me listen and smile. Only now that I know him so well as my husband do I know that his talking was nervous talking because he's a nervous flyer.

I was so relieved to get to the hotel to check in and put my feet up. I had thought I'd go change into my PJ's and watch TV like I normally do to relax after travelling. But as I turned to go to the elevator, he was there again. "Have you eaten? Would you like to go to dinner?"

And the rest is history. I was hungry after all. He was successful in getting me to go out to dinner with him because we had spent so much time chatting and getting to know each other already.
Connection. See? It sells.

Journal Assignment:

What things are important to your clients that are common ground for you?

Connection means being open with your heart. How can you be more open with your heart?

In what areas do you shield yourself from hurt? These could very well be where you can connect with your ideal client.

Why Words Matter So Much

"Words are containers for power.
You choose what kind of power they carry"
– Joyce Meyer

Remember "sticks and stones may break my bones but" …. Yeah. Well, words can hurt. We all know that.

I've always been fascinated with words, the slight difference in emotion and feeling when you use different words that are similar.

In Junior High School, we had an assignment to watch advertisements and basically tear them apart. We were supposed to listen intently to the word choices and think about how they tried to convince you to buy the product (and how well it worked).

We were also supposed to listen for stretching the truth or how different word choices could lead you to believe something without coming out and saying it.

The words that were chosen also evoked an emotion. Emotion is what gets people to buy. They see the hope in a solution. They get excited about how fun a new game is going to be. They see how they'll have better relationships with a magic pill. They look forward to satisfying their hunger with that new menu item at that cool new restaurant (add in the images and music, and there's even more emotion running through).

It was amazing to think that, in a short one minute commercial, there was probably a lot of thought put into what words were chosen to get a reaction from someone and to get them to take some sort of action.

I realized at that point how much words matter. They matter for your business too because people will get a sense of what you are about, who you are and what they can expect from your business by the words you choose.

What do you say in your conversations with people? What do you say when you write a social media post? What feeling do people get with what you say?

Words can inspire, they can empower and they can rally up. They can also tear down, deflate and ruin. You can choose to use tact and you can choose to be tactless. You can be mean or you can be nice. Which do you choose? How do you want to be perceived?

Maybe you'll recognize these words by Martin Luther King, Jr.

"Let us not wallow in the valley of despair.

I say to you today, my friends, so even though we face the difficulties of today and tomorrow, I still have a dream. It is a dream deeply rooted in the American dream.

I have a dream that one day this nation will rise up and live out the true meaning of its creed: "We hold these truths to be self-evident: that all men are created equal."

I have a dream that one day on the red hills of Georgia the sons of former slaves and the sons of former slave owners will be able to sit down together at the table of brotherhood.

I have a dream that one day even the state of Mississippi, a state sweltering with the heat of injustice, sweltering with the heat of oppression, will be transformed into an oasis of freedom and justice.

I have a dream that my four little children will one day live in a nation where they will not be judged by the color of their skin but by the content of their character.

I have a dream today."

His words have gone down in history. Inspiring. Empowering. Moving to action. This is what he's known for.

What do you want to be known for being or doing? Your words will help you achieve that. What do you want your business to be known for? Your words will help you achieve that too.

A lot of times, even though we want to be effective in our communication, it doesn't come as easy as we'd like. And it really matters in our business. If we can't say what we mean, our business suffers. We know that a confused buyer never buys, so being straightforward in your communication helps you to attract more clients.

Here are some tips to getting your point across better:

Be Clear – Be as clear as possible, using words that people will understand. Use short sentences instead of compound sentences when possible.

Be Brief - Most things can be cut by about half. Learn to love editing and cutting. Listen to what you've written with your ear, either in your head or out loud.

Simplicity – Don't use flowery language or jargon. It alienates your reader.

Humanity – Being a person is the most crucial part of your communications. When you're human, people will relate to you. When people relate to you, you have a connection. Knowing that people buy from people who they connect with, this is the most important piece to remember.

<u>Journal Assignment</u>:

How do you want to come across in life and in business? Is that different?

Have you been communicating effectively? If not, how can you improve?

How can you use words to get people interested in your business?

In what ways can you use the words you choose for good?

How are you going to change your thinking about the words you choose?

Why Your Copy has to Be THAT Good

"Our word choice gives sentences luster,
and they deserve intense attention."
- Constance Hale

Most people think of the copy they write for their business as a chore. I see is at a challenge. At each step of the way, we want something from the reader – a reaction, a feeling, an action, a yearning …. We can direct those feelings based on what we say and how we say it.

When you're an entrepreneur, choosing the words for you copy matters immensely because your copy has to be THAT good, otherwise, no one will be interested, no one will talk about you, what you say will fade away in no time and your clients won't be attracted to you. You want to be remembered.

These days, everyone is on social media. Regardless if your favorite hang out spot is Facebook, LinkedIn, Twitter, Instagram, Snapchat or whatever new one is on the horizon, we all communicate daily with writing. You might not think your posts are "copy," but they are. Communication is copy. There's usually a purpose of writing, even if the only purpose is to share something that happened today.

When you're in business, the words you use help people to see you're like them – you understand them, you relate to their struggle AND most of all, you can help them with it. You have a solution. But why would they trust you? After all, you're a stranger online to them and we're taught to distrust people.

The only way to draw people in is to use words.

My second child didn't speak for quite a long time. It wasn't until he was heading towards 3 that he decided to start speaking full sentences. My mother thought there was something wrong with him, but he was doing just fine without words before that, so I think he figured why bother?

To this day, at age 16, he's still not a kid of many words. He doesn't say much unless he decides there's a real purpose for it, he stays in his head a lot, loves robotics and is intensely mathematical and analytical. He shoots straight from the hip and just says whatever's on his mind, no fluffy extras, just the facts on a need to know basis.

The down side to this? Because he doesn't care how it comes out, and he's usually thinking only of his perspective, stuff doesn't come out right and he doesn't get the response he wants. He's not very persuasive on the parental front either.

On the other hand, he doesn't seem to mind and he's got robotics friends who understand him and speak at his level. He doesn't have any real motivation to change his communication style. When I try to talk to him about tact, word choice and explaining himself better, he looks at it as a bother.

However, as entrepreneurs, we have a lot of motivation to change our communication style if it's not working because if we don't we'll stay poor and clientless.

A while back I saw something on Facebook, an experiment of sorts to prove a point about the words we choose and how it can influence based on how we say what we say.

It was the holidays and there was a guy holding a sign asking for help. "Trying to get to CA. Need money." Not very many people helped the poor guy out.

However, when the sign was changed to "Trying to get home to CA for the holidays. Need bus fare." Guess what? People helped him. Can you see why?

First, you need to know who you are talking to. I talk to my clients about "calling in" their ideal clients. You have to define who you want to talk to before you know how to talk to them.

Think about who your ideal client is and all their qualities. Who would you LOVE to wake up and work with each and every day?

Secondly, you need to know what kind of pain they're in. Where can you help them? If they were sitting drinking coffee with their best friend pouring their heart out about everything, what would they be saying? You've got to know them at this intimate of a level.

Thirdly, put yourself in their shoes. When you were there (before you solved your struggle), what did it feel like, how would you describe that, and what would've made you feel hopeful that you could be out of that struggle?

Your marketing is only as good as your copy so your copy has to be that good. Your copy gets your ideal client to react in the way that you're expecting them to.

Each step of the way, your words in your copy attracts clients, connects with them and gets them to make that next move, whether it's to click the ad, give you their email or buy your product. Nothing can replace good copy. So make it GOOD.

Journal Assignment:

Who is your ideal client? Describe them in detail. Draw a picture of them and hang it by your desk so you see who you're talking to every day.

Put together a client checklist – who would you love to work with every single day of the rest of your life? What are they like? What qualities do they have? What are they about?

How can you improve the way you write your copy to speak directly to that client?

Want some tips to never ending content? Check out my Huffington Post article How to Consistently Create Engaging Content

http://www.huffingtonpost.com/vickie-gould/how-to-consistently-creat_b_11440324.html

Why Your Marketing Can Never End

"Consistency breeds familiarity, familiarity breeds confidence, and confidence breeds sales." – Jay Conrad, Guerilla Marketing

The day you stop your marketing efforts is the day your business ends. Few are able to stay in business without doing some sort of marketing. Even if you rely on a referral business, that is marketing – it's just that someone else is helping you to do it.

"The road to profitability is paved with credibility. Credibility is something you earn by how you market, where you market, how you treat people, how you act, and your overall level of professionalism. Away from the business arena, the term is street cred, and it's the road to respect." - Jay Conrad

What are the biggest credibility pieces that you need? Your story and your book.

Some people feel overwhelmed and confused about what to put out so they put out nothing. Some people are afraid to not be perfect enough so they hide. There are so many excuses as to why you should wait to put something out that I can't even list them all. There's just not enough room.

Here's the thing: The excuses are never valid!

Remember this if nothing else about marketing: You want your marketing to repel and attract. It's supposed to turn people off (yes, you'll get trolls and mean people commenting or responding) – those people are not meant to be in your tribe and that's so beyond fine. Do not pay them any attention or give them any time. On the flip side, the right marketing attracts your ideal client through whatever you decide to put out there.

Don't worry so much about if you look perfect, if you're saying everything grammatically correct (there are sentences in this book that aren't even real sentences!) or if you have everything ready, like websites, photos, business cards and perfect hair. If you wait until the stars all align perfectly, you'll be waiting forever.

The key to marketing is doing it consistently. Your message has to be consistent, what you're doing needs to be consistent, and who you are has to be consistent. The surest way to make someone turn around and run away is by doing one thing one day, and then doing something differently, or even in conflict the next day. They become confused and trust is lost there.

When I started my business, I was a wellness coach due to my back story and being a Master Herbalist. But I always knew I wanted to eventually be on the business side helping people grow theirs. Sales and marketing had always been an interest of mine due to my fascination with words. When I was in Junior High, I thought I was going to own an ad agency.

But the road to figuring out what kind of business coach I wanted to be wasn't that easy. In the first 10 months, I changed my mind many times. I thought I'd be a sales coach. Then I thought I'd be a media person. Then I thought I'd help people craft their story. Then I thought I'd be a mindset coach using my Law of Attraction Practitioner training.

No matter what I chose, I felt like there was a missing part. If I helped people with processes, I missed the mindset piece and if I helped people with the mindset, I didn't have the structure. I wanted something that used the feminine side and the masculine side.

Enter books for marketing. They're structured and creative, inspired and logical all at once. I was able to combine everything I wanted to help people with, all together, and it felt good. But I was still wishy-washy in my messaging.

I really loved being known for being inspiring and motivating. It felt so good. I also wanted to be known for being intelligent in my processes and strategies too. Problem was, I was scared to step out in faith that people would want all that in combination.

Then these words came out of my coach's mouth, "Vickie, you of all people should be making $10k per month. Why aren't you?" My heart sank. The answer, I really knew. I never owned what I did and I wasn't specific enough in my message. I wasn't being clear or consistent.

So I vowed to become really focused in what I was saying and in the course of the next 3 weeks, I booked 17 discovery sessions. Most weren't ideal clients, but a few were. It encouraged me to get better with my filtering process and to continue to get my message out in a way that would speak even more directly to who I wanted to work with.

I consistently showed up to social media, posting 2 times a day. My message was clear: work with me to get your book to Best Seller and then get media attention from ABC, NBC, CBS and FOX. Later I added the "after" book part of how to leverage and market your Best Seller for more impact, influence, clients and income through marketing, funnels and mindset.

Once I showed up day after day with the same message, people started to tag me in other groups as soon as the word "book" was in a post. I got referrals from people I barely knew and I woke up to messages from potential clients asking how they could work with me.

And in the next 3 months, I made over $18,000 after being what I felt like the hit and miss, accidental "one hit wonder" in all the previous months.

Journal Assignment:

Is there anything keeping you from showing up consistently, marketing your business?

In what ways can you improve your marketing?

If marketing is not something that's in your zone of genius, can you find a way to delegate it?

Why Your Feminine Side Matters So Much

"Individually and collectively, we are shifting
from a position of fear
into surrender and trust of the intuitive. The
power of the feminine energy is on the rise in
our world."
- Shakti Gawain

Calm, peace, intuition …. More moola

Until I started learning about personal
development, I never knew there was such a
thing as feminine or masculine energy. This
chapter is not just for women. Both men and
women have feminine and masculine sides
that balance each other out. The more you
can use both, as equally as possible, the
easier things are in your business and life.

All my life I'd been told to be less feminine,
that being female was a bad thing. Having
feelings was seen as weak. Leaning on
intuition wasn't smart because logic was better
since you could prove it.

When I showed up in the corporate world, in a male dominated industry filled with mathematics and computers, the more like a man I acted, the better it seemed. I learned to be tough. I was told to stop wearing my heart on my sleeve by my male boss. He even asked me, "Why do you care about everyone else so much?" I didn't understand why I shouldn't care.

I came to find out that women were seen as emotional and flighty and any time there was conflict, it was assumed to be "that time of month."

And it also wasn't really a good thing to be attractive for some reason.

As a young girl, I was taught to squelch intuition. That gut feeling that is attached to your feminine side was to be ignored because it would lead you to make a bad decision, or offend someone because there was no real evidence to back any of it up.

As a teen, I was taught to "hone in to my creeper alarm" and at the same time to be polite. The two were really in conflict. How can you be polite to someone who makes your creeper alarm go off? See how bad that situation can become because girls are taught to ignore feminine instincts?

In Asian society, having baby boys is most respected. Parents want boys.

After my older sister was born, my Dad really hoped that I was going to be a boy. Even something in the characters in my Taiwanese name was supposed to secretly indicate that I would be a boy. Well, obviously that didn't happen.

But I was supposed to be a boy. So I learned that I should be more like a boy, in thought and action, even though I loved being girly. So I decided the best thing to do was to beat out all the boys.

Whether I competed in piano, math or just plain attention, I could be better than them. I could beat them out in their job too. "Everything boys can do, girls can do better," was my motto.

The problem was that I tried to be the man in every situation, even in my marriage. I wanted to be in charge. I became the protector too.

Then I started to get really tired. It was hard to stay strong all the time, keep the emotions under control or hidden, never feel taken care of, and to always know the answers. It was exhausting. All I did was "do."

And I surely didn't know how to receive, which is a feminine thing. I wanted it in my head, but every situation that came up, I pushed away everyone's gift. I couldn't even receive a compliment without discounting it as invalid or acting like I wasn't worthy of it.

I see now that all my life I really wanted to be allowed to use that feminine side. I squelched it and ignored it even though my intuition was strong.

In entrepreneurship, there's inspired action and massive action. I'm guessing you've probably heard of these. Inspired action is feminine. Massive action is masculine.

Inspired action comes from a place where you listen to the download from The Universe or God. It's that message that you receive by faith when you ask how you can be of service. You believe that what you've been inspired with will manifest something positive for you and your business. When you're in the space of taking inspired action, you are in a place to receive.

Massive action comes from a place of masculine energy where you do a lot to get what you want. You feel fully in control of the situation and use a lot of energy to accomplish much in a short amount of time. The problem with purely relying on massive action is that you'll eventually burn out.

Massive action sometimes happens when we think of all the things we think we "should" be doing and freakishly go after it. We begin to burn the midnight oil, and then we mistakenly start to get attached to the outcome because since we've worked so hard.

Sadly, this turns into desperation. We think, "It's got to work. I've done so much." It becomes uninspired and a chore. We drag. And it's just plain yuck.

The best place to be is actually in a place of inspired massive action. This is where you've gotten an inspired download that guides you to take that massive action. The outcome is always better when you combine inspiration and action, meaning combine your feminine and masculine sides.

Journal Assignment:

In what ways have you been ignoring your feminine side?

How can you tune into your feminine side more?

Can you see how ignoring your intuition has caused issues in the past? What happened?

How can you start to combine your feminine side with your masculine side?

Can you see ways to take inspired action in your business?

What can you do daily to tune in better to both your masculine and feminine side so you can use them better?

Why Your Vibration MUST Stay High

"The Universe is not punishing you or blessing
you. The Universe is responding to the
vibrational attitude that you are emitting."
- Abraham Hicks

Maybe you've heard it before. "Be high vibe."
What does that really mean and why does it
matter?

We all have an energy about us that creates
our "vibe". Everything on earth has a
frequency, an energy signature: plants,
animals, food, etc.

You have an energy too, an aura that effects
those around you. Think about the last time
someone was grumpy around you. You
reacted, right? Sometimes those bad moods
rub off. "Misery loves company" is so true
because it just sucks you in.

When you are in that negative state, your
vibration is low. When you are in a state of
feeling grateful, worthy, and abundant, your
vibration is high. What is happening inside of
you ends up being a reflection of your outer
world.

Why does it matter? Because the Law of Attraction works whether you're consciously thinking about it or not, just like gravity. It's there and it's working regardless if we are acknowledging it or not.

If like attracts like, wouldn't you want to attract good things? Things that make you feel abundant? Using the Law of Attraction will help you to manifest what you want in your life and business and I'm not just talking about monetary goals, but people as well.

Yes, you attract the people in your life (friends and clients) and you affect them with your vibration too. You can either match theirs or they can match yours, so you might as well hang around those who are already vibrating on your same high frequency, right? That's why you hear things like, "I vibe with her." It means that you're jiving and enjoying each other's company, and your vibrational frequency is why.

Here's the thing: as with anything, applying the Law of Attraction and staying in a high vibration takes practice. There's a learning curve. You can't just announce it and have it done. You get better and better at it until it's second nature. And even then, you'll always be learning more and growing the rest of your life.

Now, don't go beating yourself up if you aren't always high vibe. It's impossible to be there all the time. Life happens. It's what you do next that matters. How long will you allow yourself to stay there? What can you do to get back to a higher vibe.

I know there are some days that are just plain non-productive, meh days. We all have them. Life is a bunch of ups and downs, like the tides we talked about before. As you practice more, you'll get better and the low vibrational times will get fewer and shorter.

Remember that you are 100% in control. The Universe and God supports you in all things always. There is always enough for you and everyone else in the world.

Journal Assignment:

If you look back in the last days or week, where have you been in high vibration?

When have you been in low vibration?

What can you do next time to change from a low vibration to a high vibration?

Look at who you surround yourself with. Is there anyone you many need to start limiting your time with?

Why Not?

"Others have seen what is and asked why.
I have seen what could be and asked why
not."
- Pablo Picasso

If you've gotten this far, you've probably
thought a couple times about not going after
it. What if it's safer to just stay where you
are?

Being comfortable is dangerous. It keeps you
small.

If you're feeling like you might like to just stay
cozy right where you are in your life and
business, ask yourself why. There's no right
or wrong answer, really but if you want
something it has to be too painful to stay
where you are or you won't budge from that
spot.

Why not?

Have you listened to all the distractions going through your head? We do such a good job convincing ourselves out of things, don't we? When, in truth, it would take less time for us to just do it than go through all the rambling thoughts about why not to do something. Are you with me?

And there's this thing called … regrets.

Why do you constantly tell yourself no? I know you do because I haven't ever met anyone who hasn't. I've done it to myself giving reasons like, "I'm too old", "my time has past", "I don't know enough", "it's selfish", "you don't deserve it", and that great and infamous, "Who are you to think you can _____?"

We've been taught to be reasonable and realistic. Keep it real, but if everyone did that, where would we be in the world? No new inventions, no new thoughts and no new learnings. Curiosity would be stifled and there would be no advancement in society. Uh-oh.

Sometimes you just have to trust your gut and take the leap. That thing that keeps coming to your mind about what you wish you could do? THAT thing is exactly what you should be doing.

When fear comes up, it tells you to run closer or run away. Depending on the situation, either is a good thing. The fears with have for our next moves in business can mean that we should run closer because fear only comes up when something is meaningful to us. We're just scared we won't get it, or worse, that we can't have it and we don't want to face that.

My mom used to always say that if you wanted to know how to do something, you could learn it. No big deal. Everything is learn-able. I think because she grew up poor, she learned to be self-sufficient and creative with what she had. She learned to do it on her own and plain figure it out.

She always said to me that books held everything and knowing how to read and understand what was written was one of the most important skills to have in life. Maybe that's why I love books so much.

As soon as Google was on the scene, I swear every question that popped into my head (and there are a lot!) about everything and anything finally had a place to go. I googled. And especially during those days I was so ill, with no set protocol and no cure, I googled a lot! Sure I had to sift through the truth and non-truth and decide, but wow, what a world opened up!

I think entrepreneurs tend to see something and say, "Hey, I can do that too!" Many of us are multi-passionate and have a ton of mad skills. I didn't realize that this mindset was different until one day my husband and I were watching the TV show called S.T.R.O.N.G. where ladies with male trainers compete against each other.

At the end of each episode, the two bottom teams compete to see who ends up getting eliminated. They go up a tower obstacle course to see who gets to the top first. Whoever gets their first wins. The other team gets eliminated.

I love these kinds of shows and one day I turned to my husband and said, I could be the lady and he could be the trainer and we could compete. He looked at me pretty incredulously and said, "I don't think so. I can't do that." (No, my husband's not a fitness trainer, he's a bean counter). I told him that of course he could and we could win.

He laughed. He said, "No way." I didn't see why not. But he did.

"If not now, when?" - Robert F. Kennedy

Most days I think I can conquer the world. I don't think there's much I can't figure out. And I have the confidence to go try, even break things in the process, learn from that and keep going until I figure it out. I'm stubborn that way. Are you?

Journal Assignment:

What kinds of things do you tell yourself no?

How are your fears keeping you small?

List out all the reasons why you should go for it.

How would it feel if you got what you wished for?

Conclusion

I see you. I hear you. You're an entrepreneur, a coach with a heart centered business. You love what you do and just want to HELP people.

What if we could turn a book .. YOUR BOOK .. into a secret weapon that would help you stand out in your industry and funnel perfect clients directly to your business?

What if your book would boost your credibility, exponentially grow your reach, improve your expert status, help you make an impact and leave behind something that really counts?

It's more than just the book though. When I help people write books, I always talk about how it parallels their business. There are great revelations and clarity that comes from organizing your thoughts in a book.

We both know that you were put on earth to be BIG and live your dream life.

So isn't it time to quit dreaming and wishing and fantasizing on how your life could be and start being the person you know you are deep inside? Wouldn't it be great to show up as YOU and be able to spread your message and mission through your coaching with your book?

I'd like to invite you now to see the possibilities. For you, your life, your family, and your future clients. What do you see? What do you write in your journal and visualize when you had no limitations?

If you'd like to finally be that person who is a world class coach with Best Selling book, take that next step. Go out in faith, knowing that you can have whatever you set your mind and heart to.

Go here to tell me more about yourself and set up a free session here: bit.ly/letstalkbook

You've got something special. That's never going to change. But if you keep it to yourself, no one else will be able to change for the better with your help.

"I had had two books, mostly written, basically sitting around doing nothing. I had no idea how to publish them or create a buzz about them once they were out. When I told Vickie about the books, she immediately asked, 'What date do you want to publish them?' and that was pretty much the start of the momentum that was created with my book and launch.

The same day my book hit international #1 best seller, I got two requests for interviews, and two clients that reached out to want to work with me. It was amazing! Since then, my expert status has grown, my credibility has been boosted and I've been able to over double my coaching package prices.

I'm forever grateful for all that Vickie's helped me with. I would be still an unpublished, unknown author if it had not been for her coaching."

~ Karen Donaldson, Executive Public Speaking Coach, Certified Confidence and Self Leadership Coach, International Speaker

"I fall into the category of someone who has been wanting to write my book for a long time now. My book is part of my story and part of me and that's why it's really meaningful for me.

What really helped me was getting really clear on my why and thinking beyond the book. It made me realized that writing my book is a stepping stone to a longer process of growing and marketing my business. That was a turning point for me.

A light bulb went off one day when I was trying to shift into something that felt good for my book. I needed more connection to my own calling and my desires. When that became evident to me, my message and content in the book became perfectly in alignment with what I want to do.

Then the marketing part of what Vickie taught me took the book to a whole new level. The biggest epiphany for me was when I started to tell people I was writing the book and I realized just how clear the message needed to be. Once I hit that milestone of clarity, I had the clear direction I needed to I to knock out most of my book easily."

~ Andy Smith, Spiritual Entrepreneur and Mindset Coach

Wouldn't you love to finally say, "Yes" to yourself? No more rationalizations about why you're not enough, you don't deserve it, it's not for you or it won't work out. ***No regrets.***

It's time to take the leap. It's time to take a chance on your true desires. It's time to step into being the true to yourself.

You know you have a message for the world and you know you weren't put here to be mediocre. I know that too.

It's time to go here to tell me more about yourself and have your free call with me:
bit.ly/letstalkbook

About the Author

Vickie Gould is an international coach, author and speaker. She's been seen on ABC, NBC, CBS and FOX and has written multiple #1 Best Selling books and helped others to do the same. In doing so, she's helped entrepreneurs to grow their businesses through their increased expert status. She helps them to become who they've always dreamed of becoming with a thriving business that supports the freedom-based lifestyle they were meant for.

She lives in Michigan with her husband and 3 children.

Her background includes:

- Law of Attraction Certified Practitioner through Global Sciences Foundation
- Certified Divine Living Transformational Life and Business Coach through Divine Living Academy, ICF approved for specific coaching hours

- Silver Protégé Sales Certified through Eric Lofholm International
- Completed programs from and trained with Brian Tracy, Brendon Burchard, Tony Robbins, Ted McGrath, and Callan Rush
- Studying NLP through Global Science Foundation
- Publisher and Owner of Real Deal™ Magazine
- Master Herbalist, Reiki Master, Aromatherapist.

Visit her at www.vickiegould.com and join her Facebook group at www.facebook.com/groups/betherealdeal

www.ingramcontent.com/pod-product-compliance
Lightning Source LLC
Chambersburg PA
CBHW070040210526
45170CB00012B/554